Lovers in Evolution

Lovers in Evolution

Carolyn Mary Kleefeld

Prologue,
Collaboration in Editing and Organization
by Patricia Karahan

THE HORSE AND BIRD PRESS   LOS ANGELES

The following poems have been printed in the publications listed: "From the heat a dryness rises" (*American Poetry Anthology*); "The golden egg flames on," and "Beyond the sight of eye" (*C.S.P. World News-Canada*); "The unseen God does live" (*Monterey Peninsula Herald*); "And if you can not, all else is less than what Is," "You were the summer, long before the Summer came," and "In fevered light" (*Satan Sleeps With the Holy: Word Paintings*). "A shadowed Religion of Being" was awarded honorable mention in the Southern California Poets Pen Competition.

Other books by Carolyn Mary Kleefeld:
Published by The Horse and Bird Press

Climates of the Mind
Hardbound Limited Edition,
   signed and numbered   1979
Softbound, now in its third printing   1979

Satan Sleeps With the Holy: Word Paintings
Hardbound   1982
Softbound   1982

Our continuing deep appreciation to Ginger Huston for her invaluable assistance. Our acknowledgment to the Palomar and Lick Observatories, to NASA, and to Robert Burnham, Jr. for permission to use their photographs. Mr. Burnham's photographs first appeared in *Burnham's Celestial Handbook, Vol. 3,* Dover Publications, Inc. Special thanks to Becky Goodman.

Front Cover: Composite photograph of Earth rising behind the moon, with the sun's rays at Earth's edge. NASA.
Back Cover: The sun and the moon's surface. From NASA photographs.

Library of Congress Card Catalogue Number: 83-082753
ISBN: 0-9602214-0-9

Printed November 1983 in the United States of America

Published by The Horse and Bird Press
Post Office Box 67C89, Los Angeles, California 90067

In reverent and honorary acknowledgment
to my discreet Muse
from whom my life is inseparable
and without whom
Lovers in Evolution
would not have come into being

When ideas are formed,

grow bodies,

join the living

The guardian to whom

they are entrusted is

of the essence of importance

Thus *Lovers in Evolution* is dedicated to

Patricia Karahan

who communed with

each new life

with the rare and sacred

integrity of her vatic senses

Contents

III. TRANSITION

IV. EVOLUTION

Prologue

To embody evolution is to unify the finite and the infinite. One is then borne by an ennobling tension, an exquisite balance which engenders consummate freedom.

Duality becomes illusion; intuition inspires perception; the subjective enhances the objective. Desire, ignited internally by this inherent power, yearns beyond the bounds of self; sensing the enigmatic, all that is vague, changing, becoming. Life is lived at the subtle edges, in visceral cohabitation with the unknown, extending one's sensual and conceptual horizons. Finite and infinite continuously refine dimension. In this expansion, one aligns with the forces of the universal order.

Life which so embodies evolution, in turn impels essential art. Such art contains the genesis of this vital force, its rhythms; goes beyond the temporal; fulfills an intention of Nature.

And, as philosopher-poet Carolyn Kleefeld so lives, so she imparts, in *Lovers in Evolution*, this essential art: the grandeur of the legendary.

Patricia Karahan
Venice, California
October, 1983

The tapestry of the Infinite
Its integral threads interwoven,
Is the sublime in undesign;
The vast microcosm of math,
Yet the extreme simplicity of
The ultimate equation
Truth equals Life

Lovers in Evolution

LOVE

Passion and Nature are of one force;
Their Life propelled by the essential will of
Movement – change – evolution

Nebulous Star Cluster M16 in Serpens, Palomar Observatory photograph.

To make of the love that unshadows the moon

You lie on a white beach
In your white slacks
And the command,
The insistence of
Your intensity,
Your muscular silence
Speaks of an urgency
Of a desire
To make love . . .

To make of the love
That unshadows the moon
The red love
That inflames the mind
Soaring it
Beyond this sun

The making of a love
That swirls
Our two planets
To a further constellation
Of our selves

This insistence of
Your intensity
This muscular silence
That speaks in urgency
Behind your white clothes
Commands the desire
For this kind of love

A shadowed Religion of Being

In roseate hues
Of candle's light
I see you, rose-lit
Reclined on damask sheets

A shadowed
Religion of Being
Night-eyed, night-haired
Your black intensity inflamed
In glowing tones

You embody
Those paintings of
Centuries ago
Your portrait illumined
By flickers
Of candle's life

And as the shadows
Incarnate their spirits
Upon your lean canvas
Your flushed darkness
Envelops, holding still my shadows –
A bone-less blending of us, into you

We breathe
Our sleep inward
As one . . .
And in the last flutter
Of candle's light,
We sink in dream
This night

Of the living of us

Connecting to invisible currents
A vast empyrean network
Connecting to every stream, vein
Connecting me to myself
Yet to All . . .
Lying in the breezes
Cross-currenting breezes roam the house
Through the doors, windows
From your still mobility
Living so largely
Next to me
Warm in a distant coolness
I feel your large bones
Without touching them
Your marrow yields to mine
A silent fever inter-mixes
Our currents mesh
Propelling flight – vision
Connection to stars
They fall into our bed
They lie around and under us, uncrushed
Whole – luminous horizons – pulse
The Unknown breathes closer
In our revolving expansion
The moon that has not yet risen
Coolly pillows my glowing head
And the sun that has long set
Radiates from the life
Of the living of us

In the galaxy of us

Are you assured
When we are distanced – that
We'll be together again?

When the seas of you are restless
Demanding storm,
Yearning a new moon of me
To soothe your tides
Begin again . . .

Are you assured
From a distance – that
We'll be together again?

And when your sun
Lights alien earth
Bruising your eyes;
Your rays bouncing back, unmet –

Are you assured
From a distance – that
We'll be together again?

Do you know
We live in each other's orbit
My earth and moon
Revolve your sun
Your beams root,
Green my gravity
And through your light
I see my moon

Knowing this you must be assured
That even when we are distanced
We are together
In the galaxy of us
Revolving on

The purple serpent pleads for more

Urgency breathes away my air
Breathless, I around me peer
Yet it is within me
That the serpent coiled,
Begins to move in a restless lure

I attempt to lock my chamber door
And soothe my pink velvet floor
But bearing up under my very core
The purple serpent pleads for more

The serpent now has recoiled throughout
I've become his chambered night
His scented flames are in my breath
He's swallowed the key to my chamber door

You visit from unrealized realms

How dare you be
A visitor
Unto me –
My home

How dare you visit
My mind
Soaring me beyond
Where others go

How dare you visit
My hidden caves
Currenting tides
To oceanic rise,

My chambers
Not the same
For receiving you

How dare you be
A visitor
Yet one
Who can live
Full moons with me . . .

Upon this planet Gaia
You visit from unrealized realms
You see from upper spheres
How fallow the soil for
Your walk

When you visit me
You embody me –
Have a home
Within me

And with you
I have a visitor
Of the unrealized realms

And if you can not, all else is less than what Is . . .

When you come to me,
Bring me not, flowers grown of my garden

When you come to me,
Bring me not
The stars off the jasmine vine
But those living in your eyes

When you come to me,
Sperm my eyes with galaxy's light

The star of me rests on the mountain top
I hear the sea's melodic voice below
Its tidal-chant pulses
Refilling my moon-pools . . .
Remoleculed

When you come to me,
Bring your own sea
Your own tides, currents

When you come to me,
Garland my waiting necks
In coils of your humid breath

continued

And to my openings
Ecstasy your pollen
We then be
Infused mutants
Of each other

And tonight the full moon
Reflects platinum undulations
Of the planet-seas

Come to me
With your own full moon
Your own planet

And if you can not
All else
Is less than
        What Is . . .

of Yarn

We weave a fabric of us
Tight and strong
Our hammocks had been to- and fro-ing,
Far too long
The threads chosen were of our fibers,
Only the staunchly pure were strung

Spinning backward all around us
Is the planet's mismatched yarn
Shuffling a wake
Of dust trailing on

Of the command of desire

The command of desire
Lifts my embrace — upward,
Into yours

Your dark humidity smolders,
Exudes a pervading sultriness
Your velvet clime enveloping — consumes,
Emblazons my titian hues

Your countless fingers
Magnetic in endless touch
Opiate an abandon
A spell-lavished ecstasy . . .

Currented fingertips of rain
Chime across my redwood roof
Resounding our sublimity
In scintillating tune

In tune as with our touching
In tune as with our rising
Fluid as in our merging
As in our orchestration
Of the command of desire

Another kind of heat

Gazing into
The sun's warming eye
At the end of day
I'm caught a-light
By its radiant beams
Hair, skin, with glint of kiss —

You drink in my heated light
Consuming the sun who has loved me;
My lover and I

You swallow my intoxication
Into your olive self
Incensing your humid sleekness
Your ignited loins uncoil,

Serpentine in movement
You wind me in rapture;
Your enveloping atmosphere

Another kind of heat
Is now our aphrodisiac

You were the summer, long before the Summer came

You were the summer, long before the Summer came,
Whilst the rains teemed through light and dark
Resounding the eternal water chimes
Upon my redwood roof —

You were the summer, long before the Summer came,
Entering my redwood home
Of blazing hearth
You brought another fire, Smoldering
Behind your meteorites of eyes

You were the summer, long before the Summer came,
Your solar flames uncoiled
As thirsty serpent tongues — Abound
Lapping my hair, my air
Consuming my winter lakes
The climate changed

You were the summer, long before the Summer came,
Your long beamed fingers flew
Their currents through
Remolding the multi-spheres of me

You were the summer, long before the Summer came,
Soaring to a weightless realm
We are beyond any Time
                    Of year

Within each other's wilderness of selves

We lived inside each other
For these fluid days and nights
Where time and sun
Were lived in
By the others

Our wicks ignited
By our sinuous flames
We were magnetically drawn – Transfixed
Beyond our eyes
To each other

Our burgundy shadows
Urged silence to pulse –
Our murmuring loins to fuse
Beyond selves

Curtains stayed closed
The vast blazon sky was inside
Our sensibilities breathed deeply, Of
The clime in each other

The wilderness of ourselves
Wove a kingdom mounted high
In languor we were silked
Our opiate was enrapture

There were no walls or doors
Nor recognizable rooms
Only in our woven kingdom
May we be contained – Untamed
Within each other's wilderness of selves

In fevered light

O the fog-filled face of you
Blends with the clouded skies
You drift in the foggy dusk
As another sphere of mist

Through dark glistening eye
Your humid clime envelops me
As the lowered sky

Only our fevered beams
Burn through this sunless hour
And so light the heavy mist
Of an ended day

You of black moon
Penetrate the dark
With fixed raven eye

Your night imbibes my dusk
We walk home over
Unseen meadows

Our heavy sultry blood
Moves us quickly
In fevered light

The incubation of our heat

The golden egg
Of my sun within
Bursts, exploding
Shoots of violet,
Fuchsia, maize –
The wildflowers of me
Match the musky hills
Wilderness inhales me,
My skin is flowered
I travel down the beams of me
To the Aegean seas below
Where I'm naked to all
To the sands, tides, love –
The love that pollinates your eyes
The stems of our wildflowers entangle
I'm drawn to your stamen,
Your core of honey
Our limbs shade us from the other sun
As we bathe in each other's honey;
The incubation of our heat

Beyond the sight of eye . . .

O timeless eyes
Of nut-gold black
In day's light
You blaze as suns
Your boldness sparks
Metallic flight

In the flat of shade
And hueless night
Your sentient suns
Darken, cool
Their blaze molten
To a cobalt black

O meteoric eyes
Of Mercury borne
You transform — transport me
Into your timeless night

Behind your eyes, empyrean
I breathe now of your mind's vision
I see beyond the sight of eye
Needing not of any light

We are rays to the future

Discovering an intimate cove;
A realm awakened
Realizing the island today,
Of each other
The sphere in which we both can thrive
Apart and within each other
Envisioning the island of us —
Pristine of sand
Opaline of sea
Contained within
Yet linked to All
Our atmosphere unfurling
Flighting our wingéd bond of vision
Our sands sculpting our island
The circulation of us
Currenting the tides that define, refine —
Our ideology evolving,
Crystallizing jade and amethyst rocks
On which to rest, ponder
Beaming fully in the present,
We are rays to the future

NATURE

To grow deep within Nature's roots,
To breathe the rhythms of her breath
Is to live in God's possession

Jupiter in Taurus, a composite photograph by Robert Burnham, Jr.

The golden egg flames on

O gardens of the birds in paradise
At last I nest in you
In the destined seed of pollination,
In the fervid symphony
Of roots in flight

O ever-brimming bounty of Design
Pulsing scent and bud divine
The jasmine vine lace-veils my roof
Its fragrant stars fall wet-lashed in storm
Glistening an intimacy to my closed door

O cerulean skies of quixotic mood
You bow low in rain and sun
And in love's full-mooned eye
You marry these gardens
Of the birds of paradise,

Moistening with dewy lips
Your bride's eternal births
Woo-ing in lulling breeze
The unfolding of her glowing lids
In emerging dawn

And on and on
The honey fills
The golden egg flames on

And all of whom these gardens sing
Wed to the unity
Of the Heavens and the Gardens
Of the birds in paradise

From the heat a dryness rises

From the heat a dryness rises,
The moist green leaves and ferns of Spring
Bordering the canyon roads
Are masked now in settled clay
Of the Summer's dust

From the heat a dryness rises,
Passion's fire births the ash's dust
In the hearths of those who've breathed
The life of limbs and mind a-flame

From the heat a dryness rises,
Life diffused; Blurs
As dust adrift
Masking leaf and trunk
The Eye of man

From the heat a dryness rises,
A season changes
Moisture may return to marrow
Clay to its earth
And the dust of dryness may settle
On the roads

But not for the human spokes on wheels

Of the religion of nature

Enshrouded in gossamer sheaths
Of a twilight fog
A statuesque grove of Eucalyptus
Bathes in gauze of mist

Blurry in twilight dim
This silvery-green sanctuary stands
Imbuing the scent of eternal root

Sinuous loins of massive trunk
Sculpt in ceaseless rise
Revealing bare limbs of
Antler bones a-spire;
A colossal herd of leafed deer in grove

Dappled faces shimmering lift
Unbound to skies in unheard song

Stars fruit an evening bloom;
White suns of night incense with light

Silent incantations verse
Of the religion of nature

The maestro's orphic state

Last night
The wind in an orphic state
Bellowed its tempestuous senses out,
Lifting the heavy weight
Of gray sleep;
Whirling the Spirits' yesterdays
Through the howl of jet-currented tunnels
Beyond the black void —
Out through gilded portals high
Where their eyes rejoice to open

The next morning rests in calm
All that can be seen, of
The maestro's orphic state
Is without the use of mortal shears,
The summer's hair is shorn —

Its dryness blown has fallen,
Brown-carpeting the green whispers
Of winter's dewy sprouts

Beyond dark Eagle clouds

Colossal Eagle wings of clouds
Feather the wilderness of sky

Dark and great they quicken —
Scavengers of light

The last thin flame
Of sun's descent
Is quenched in liquid dark

These night flocks of Eagle clouds
These great dark wings of night
Migrate farther still
Spread larger in wind's flight

Necks stretched long
Through airy fields
They're harbingers of night

And suddenly through a flocked black wing,
The night as its ebony brow
Dazzling streams of phosphorous beams
Stare, from the full brazen Eye

This luminous oracle sees
Beyond dark Eagle clouds
All there Is to know

That which is necessary to you

Like a cormorant
You sail
Dry of shiny feather
Sleek, jet-bodied
You're curved for speed
You poise
Eyes scope-sighted
Focusing on your prey;
That which is necessary to you

And you swoop it up
Your meal
Devouring, diffusing it
Only the eyes watch . . . awhile
The rest dissolves in the abandon
Of exquisite pain

In the intimacy of cove

In the ebony of night
In the fathomless seas below
An intimate cove is slept in
By many a fishing boat

They breeze in at the dusky hours
To sleep on her wide sleek bed
Their amber lamps
Cast shimmering paths
Reflecting her rhythmic swells

The men rest deep in a seminal sleep
In the black of her liquid sheets
In the intimacy of cove

And eager in the first yawn of light
They alert to heave their nets
Splashing aside her azure sheets
Deep through to her teeming belly

And swiftly then they scurry
Securely tying their rig
Promptly to sell her bounty
The freshness of their catch!

The unseen God does live

Contained in the raging force
Of a thunderous stallion-surf
The endless tides of freedom churn
The unseen God does live

Contained in the orange poppy
The unseen God does live
Its wild bud unfurls to flower
The vivid heralding of Spring

Contained in the human Spirit
An unseen God does live
Guarding the fires of Living
Stoking Truth's incessant flame

A gentle rain softly moistens
Blossoming an early Spring
The potent skies are flooded gray
The unseen God does live

My Muse; Poetree

Serendipity
visited me
this noon
as I happened
to sit
beneath a particular tree

My pen
wouldn't write
My paper
was bored
Then suddenly
garlands of boughs
seemed to embody me
sprouting verse
that in truth
quite astonished me!

Then star-shaped leaves
would begin to fall
whenever a word was amiss
If a dot was left off
even a seed
would soon drop
filling the space
in Poetree

I must have breathed
the same breath
as this tree
as I can't
distinguish
it
from
me

The innocent mauve of dawn

From the heaviness
Of a sleeping house

Wingéd senses draw me out
To the innocent mauve of dawn

I seem to rise
Off the edge of Earth
Communing with
The galactic realms

My inner rows of candles lit
In this innocent mauve of dawn

Amidst the fade of mercurial spheres
Spiraling stars can still be seen
Tumbling into slumbering hills
In the innocent mauve of dawn

And o'er the velvet mountain high
A hovering bride of moon
Ephemeral in illumined gown
So hesitates in morning's path, as
Her radiant groom ascends

And so moves on . . .
The innocent mauve of dawn

In séance with the earthly wilds

After the heavens' wilderness storms
The night sky clears
In this empyrean lake of dark
The full moon soars,

The earthly wilds are summoned to séance
Embodied in diaphanous beams
Entranced by possessing shadows;
In the lurking of their urge

This night – the dawn,
Cast distant
From a stranger's light

The heavens root gold

Here on Earth
In this rooted wilderness
Of meadow
The heavens have lifted
Gardens to paradise

In these gardens so enchanted
Thrive scented galaxies
Golden globes of flower
Warm the eye
As suns –
Gild the soul
As Gods

From the wilds' cerulean aviary
Astral voices trill elysian songs
The meadows ascend
On pollination's wing

Archways vined of bended bough
Petaled in pastel, of
French countryside faces
Nod an invitation intimate
To those whose spirits move
To the fertile rhythms of timelessness

These gardens so enchanted
Brim of bursted seed
Now to dry in summer
Their perpetual hearts will seed
A meadow-paradise

The heavens root gold
In this earthen sky

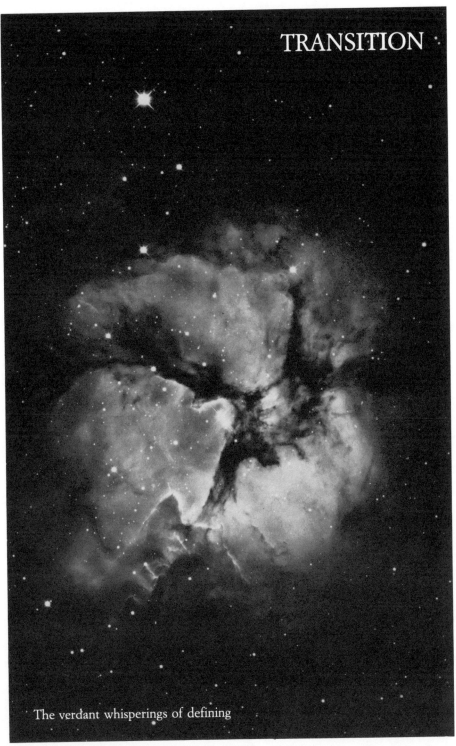

TRANSITION

The verdant whisperings of defining

The Trifid Nebula, Lick Observatory photograph.

A dark shade of flower grows

Deep within the marsh of you
From your earth's bowels
Lives the bromeliad of you —
And from the vortex
of your plant
A dark shade of flower grows
Its root is of your blood
Your climate — its air
It breathes of both of you
And its aroma
Reels me in
Into the suction of you
Into your whirlpool currents
Drawing in my translucent wings
They limp —
Without their flying-dust,
Fold
Inside you

In Doubt . . .

For the bride who marries
In Doubt –
When she says "Yes"
She also says "No"
Her selves so divorced
Can't marry

For the bride who marries
In Doubt –
Wears an uncleanable gown
Its cumbersome train gathers dust
As she glances to view
Where she's been

Her hesitant veils never lift
Permanently draped
From the wind

For the bride who marries
In Doubt –
Wears gloves which reach out to hello
As permanently part of her skin

For the bride who marries
In Doubt –
When she says "Yes"
She also says "No"

A perennial bride, Yet
Long married, to
Her persistent suitor . . .
                    Doubt

And the past is carried to sea

The world's tourists
Having left the tread of their imprints —
Patterns alien and irregular
Upon the public beach of me
Now in the surge of tide
Leave my sands unmarked

My memory's eye
Once framed by the clutter of
Trash cans brimming
With vacant containers;
Reminders of consumption
Now in the surge of tide
Washes away the meaningless

The parking lot of me
Once vacated in darkness,
Over-used in sun's light
Now in the surge of tide
Is washed away

And the past is carried to sea . . .

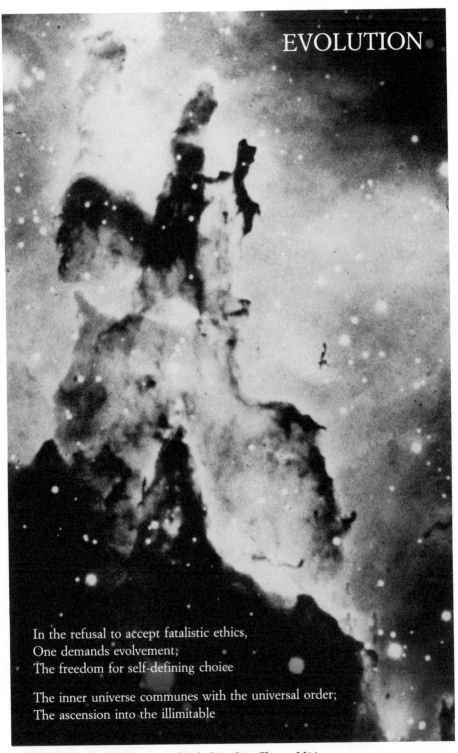

EVOLUTION

In the refusal to accept fatalistic ethics,
One demands evolvement;
The freedom for self-defining choice

The inner universe communes with the universal order;
The ascension into the illimitable

The Star Queen, central feature of Nebulous Star Cluster M16,
print enlarged by Robert Burnham, Jr.

The timeless scrolls of DNA

Within one's molecular labyrinths . . .

Atomic ladders:
The timeless scrolls
Coiled within – Unwind
Filial threads unfurl
Spiral above the bind of gravity
Commute the contained heat of the invisible
Evolving self
Transmuting one to All
Transmitting All to One

Atoms mirror atoms

Leaving the body
Abandoning the finite,

An evolving-revolving vessel
Transmitting pulse from every pore
The ignited senses;
Electrically charged antennae
Laser threads mercurial
Connecting, fusing
A triumphant penetration
Through Time – Space
Beyond the present – gravity

A personal planet evolving – emerges – Merging
The vessel, the vehicle
Breathes the wing span of the Universe
Living immeasurable vision

Mobilizing another center,
Another gravity
Revolving in one harmony
With the universal order,

The sublime network;
An order interrelating
All to All

In the profound meaning of Integration
Marrow incenses marrow
Atoms mirror atoms –
Magnetic pools of eternal eloquence
In fathomless silence
So speak

Conversation = less

What is it that we can not hear
In the birds chirruping
Is their song
More than all our words

Or is it in the wingéd Life
That All is said . . .

The inaudible All
Conversation = less

In commemoration of Rilke and Rodin:
The will of the interior voice

From the gravity of my alien earth
The umbrageous urge gestures
Drawing me, armfolded, into myself
I — my body curve inward,
Contoured to womb
To the ever fecund depths of solitude

To my settled seeds
Their bud faces yet unseen
To my mist-veiled landscapes
Where clouds drift on — revealing
Sculpted alcoves sprouting, flourishing
Without my conscious care
To the ceaseless wilderness of me
Stretching beyond eye — to vision

My dawn's lashes open
Widening to lucid eye
The morning's radiance illumines
Swallowing the night's shadows
As unneeded blankets cast off

My soul is in luminescence draped

The constant umbrage of will urges —
The unfurling ascendance of origin gestures
Some linger submerged, partially veiled in yesterday's foam;
Others, their forms defined from my tides, rise
Having veined of my streams
They demand present life — *continued*

Beseeching my breath
To blood their organs,
Embody their legends; history
Germinate myself, them, my alien earth
With the pulse of the fever that chills;
The vatic senses of white heat,

Be without garments, scorched
In deserts where the blanched bones of
Lament and longing anchor a drought

Borne then by insistent winds
Myth is outlived
As erosion moves the blocking boulder,
History is dead
Buried with indifference

Emerald seeds are set free
Gliding balms of breeze to inception
Lost to sight
Regained in vision
As now on this golden mound of meadow
In Light's day